decomposition

decomposition: poems on the ecology of trauma

by Maggie Bowyer

Copyright © 2025 by Maggie Bowyer

All rights reserved. No part of this book may be reproduced in any manner whatsoever without written permission except in the case of brief quotations embodied in critical articles and reviews and certain other noncommercial uses permitted by copyright law. For permission requests, write to the author at the email address below.

Maggie Bowyer
Raleigh, North Carolina
www.maggiebowyer.com
hello@maggiewrites.com

ISBN: 9798987027745
Printed in the United States of America
First Printing, 2025

crows hold grudges for 17 years
after Cat Speranzini

the clock restarts each time I catch
an accidental glimpse in the mirror -
      green eyes,
      a pronounced cupid's bow
      stands out against
      alabaster skin,
      a patch of freckles
      the same double-bracket
      collar bones peek out
      of her hand-me-down
      cardigan
my mother's ghost greets me
in the morning, brushing my tender
teeth, enamel eroded by a decade
without dental care. my tongue
travels over rough fillings and
receding gums, wondering how
long until I, too, need a crown.
when my nail beds bleed,
I envy her steroid-induced talons;
at what point did I learn to flinch
from my mother's touch?
my fascia is made of trigger points,
tension and resentment
I am a body created to recoil.
crows care for the injured
members of their flock, but

even they know a fledgling with
      clipped wings
will only ever know suffering.

another season's end

The dying breath of autumn screams
      Please! Stay!
Even as they watch the last leaf turn.
      Daddy! Come quickly!
Those few extra seconds of shivering.
        She's not gone!
        Not gone! She's not
        Gone!
I love you I know I love you I know
I love you I love you I love you know
I love you my father's whispered apologies
get lost in the trees of my grief.
The Solstice sings softly
      each season will get better,
      and worse.
Still   she ushers in winter.

Winter Took More Than She Needed

The last of my dwindling garden.
      A mother's life.
The creek, permanently dried up.
      A mother's life.
The batch meals from before the snow.
      A mother's life.
The peach trees in the backyard.
      A mother's life.
The ever-dwindling cash supply.
      A mother's life.
The remnants of our love affair.
      A mother's life.

I read this poem to my therapist

The words   *I'm dissociating*   get lost in the
foggy forest
my fingers numbly thumb for the phrase
but the Raynaud's makes it difficult
to hold anything close in this cold.   *I'm sorry.*
I let you down
and this apology crashes through the tree branches
but doesn't reach the sky.   I know I'm getting
worse again
I know I'm getting worse again
I know I'm getting worse again,
again,
again,
I am tumbling through the underbrush
the main trail is swarming with screaming faces
in place of tree stumps, all the side paths have become
overgrown,
unused after a harsh winter
I scare off every soft prey in my radius,
I am terrifying myself, stuck in
a frigid blizzard
(am I stranded or am I the storm?)

The words are stuck and ~~I am standing in the kitchen~~
in the middle of the woods   and   I cannot tell you
I am screaming   I'M DISSOCIATING
but
I cannot make my frostbitten lips obey
I AM SORRY

caged

In dreams, your golden hands
are covered in charcoal.

You draw me,   crushed
between the dresser and the bed,
my whimpers nearly audible.
My limbs are tangled,
tear tracks trailing down my arms.
You plant gardens
      on the periphery,
          coax me out like
the wounded animal I have become.
I wrench myself into waking

only to find my palms coated
in pomegranate juice, the anthocyanins
staining everything a deep red.
The garden beds are overflowing with
milkweed and beauty;
      blood is all I see.

I pace like the caged animal I have become.

There are claw marks on   the door frame,
                                  the walls,
                                  my arms.

The swirling crimson covers everything.

Poppies fill the front lawn, blooming
ahead of the chrysanthemums, and
I have to wonder if I am summoning
                                      Death.
Maybe I am hoping to sidetrack Him
with the scenery.

In dreams, you cradle my corpse inside
your chest cavity, staving off the stench
until you can bury me in a field of sun lilies.
You plant gardens on the periphery,
a sanctuary for my specter.
I thrash through ephialtes,   but
you have done all you can for me.

What if this soft body is prey?
after Mary Oliver

You catch my scream,
your fingers caressing
my esophagus;
they come away bloody.
Is that not your tender point?
                    you croon.
The soft body of this animal
                craves
the clutches of sharp teeth.
I spent months circling
my enclosure, snapping
at every passerby, only
to wonder why no one
released me. You lurked
just out of my jaw's reach,
                  whispering
don't bite the hand wound
around your survival.
The soft body of this animal
thirsts for retribution; apologies
aren't enough, I want to eat
your innards raw.
The vultures
will be here soon, regardless.

Scavenger

iron and rust permeate the air,
a trail of blood leads the wolf to
                bone bent, skin
                    broken.
the predators did not pick
the body clean, leaving scavengers
a whimpering feast. the animal
prods for the wound, the sand
soaking up the carnage too slowly.
claws slice through sinewy tissue,
the starving creature clamoring for
purchase   gnawing
                    at the
                    remains

    gorging

    in a way
      only
    someone
    who can't
    remember
    their last
      meal
     would
  understand

<u>I am terrified of weather because
I see you when it rains</u>
after Noah Khan

your ever-shrinking form smoking on the front porch,
cell phone in the crook of your shoulder

profanities pouring from your puckered lips,
   cigarette butt pinched between your
      fingers.
I close all the blinds but still hear your rage
   pitched above the thunder.
the back deck is drenched but my deft feet
   slip across the planks,
towards the protective foliage of the forest.
the storm kicks up Her feet in protest, the wind
   delivering your wails to me.
the tepid lake swallows my shins before I register the
   body of water.
 even submerged, the squalls ripple across the
   inland sea,
 sending shudders through me.
a drowning man will clutch at a straw
 I wring myself out then walk
   back towards the house

<u>humans can see more shades of green
than any other color</u>

and she is refracted
in each hue.

the ferns she lovingly tended,
how we all stretched towards her.

forests flashing by, how my heart
still tries to outrun the anger.

the moss walls crush themselves
closer, how intimate a room becomes

when you push on pale green bruises,
how we all flinched away from her.

until death

use my fingers as a toothbrush,
my distal bones gliding over
your gums (how you loved to
      feel me in your mouth).
mount my ribs in the entryway;
slam the front door! I will clasp
your jacket between bits of cartilage.
this is your first appearance in weeks,
the door frame shuddering.
my carcass welcomes you home,
the dried-out leather of my skin
caressing your decaying form.
my clavicle scrapes against
the diner plate, and you choke
on leftover ligaments (let me be
      the last thing you taste).

My Fingers Ache From Holding On

slick and heavy,
there is nothing to grip   except memories
(clinging,
clinging).
white caps crash over the deck,
sweeping my feet along with the current (again
again).
flashes of red bring me back to myself -
hanging onto the mast   my fingers raw
my mother beside me   clawing.
she rips at my tattered clothes,
lashing out at my face (once more,
once more).
even tethered to her,
I cannot fight a squall
(finally, something is dead to me)
hands cramping,   arms aching,
appendages shriveled,
entire body shaking

I am alive

when the rain slows,
flooded   yet
alive.

the water swallowed her readily

but the sea
spit me out.

the hands that feed me

the satisfying tear of flesh / the soft give of muscles and tendons under gnashing / teeth sink into arteries / *this is unadulterated power* / soiled, vacant eyes, and broken bones bulge against bloodless skin / the *crunch* of your kneecap punctures the quiet / my blood-filled body still bruises / brain cells are active for several minutes (sometimes hours) after death / your sagging lips beg /
my fingers pry your jaw open and stuff your mouth with pomegranate seeds / *taste every bite, my darling*

Roadkill

snow lulls my foggy mind into
      burning dreams
the sheets of ice swaddling
      my exposed organs.
everything is cold, numb after
      hours spent
      screaming
      at the storm.
grainy images, framed by a vignette
      capture   my fleeting
        attention,
      and I am swept into the dark.
a low snorting wakes me, a damp nose
burrowing in my ear, sniffing my neck;
      the wolf   finds
        the mutilation.
      they tug at the edges,
        their muzzle
        widening
        the gap
        between
me   and   survival.
the animal crawls into the cavern
they carved,   a contented
  rumble reverberating through
      my carcass.
the morning finds us   surrounded,
birds picking at bloodless skin.

the wolf rises, not satiated, the cloying
in their gut,   demanding
                they
        protect the prey
     feast on the competition
their canines flashing once white
                        then crimson,
                   maroon,
       even a corpse
       cannot see through
       such violence.
their body, slick with gore,
presses against my stiff form,
their teeth gnawing my forearm,
seeking comfort in desecration.

I forgive the animal   who
makes use   of the leftovers.

<u>predator</u>

I curl your corpse
into the crook of my arm,
lull you gently to sleep
  (the gash in your throat
  bleeds into me, slowing
  until we are matted together.
  I lap at the wound, savoring
  the last taste of you on my lips).
I dig my fingers into
the decaying skin of your neck,
thrust you off of me, then lick
each of my appendages clean.
  You're stuck
  in my bite,
  the gap between
  my front teeth.
I wipe my lips, smearing
crimson across the scene
  (my arms ache
  with restraint,
  a knife sliced
  against my palm,
  fingers twitching
  towards your
  prone figure).
There is not enough time
before sunrise

(*it's blue hour* and
your warm hands
are still in my lap).

When I turn to leave,
I don't say anything
>   (*wouldn't want to
>   wake the ghosts*
>   and your hands
>   are cold).

On dying

At first, you don't feel the reaper's grip
(only the current pulling you deeper)
the turbulence increases,	waves of nausea,
	you briefly contemplate rip tides.
two weeks go by before you dial the doctor
because you have lived plenty long underwater.
frothing at the mouth, you mumble
your manifestations into the ether and
they tell you to drag your water-logged body
	up the beach and	to the hospital
floating through the check-in,	you wait
	twelve hours for them to wring you out.
barnacles cover your skin and the seaweed
flows relentlessly, yellow-green rivulets
streaming from your stomach.
the reaper hovers in the corner	*a mirage,* they
say
	we're headed to the shore,
	they reassure you.
over the next four days,	you watch
the sun from beneath the water. the dappled light
burns, but they pump you full of fluids.
the reaper hides in the adjoining bathroom,
	gloating.
when they discharge you, the concrete
stings like hot sand on bare feet;
you squint through clear eyes

(your body still feels submerged and
your throat aches from
all the salt water you swallowed).

no one mentions the reaper following you home

all I ask is for you to spread my ashes in the Atlantic

Since   tearing
out of my mother's womb,
I have been filled with
a violent longing,
palms smacking into the ceiling.
My   need   permeates
every sense   (where should I place
               my blood-soaked feet?)
Crack open my chest and
you will find   crabs
                 skittering across
                 marshy wetlands, crashing
                 and clashing; in the corner,
                 one crustacean
                 cannibalizes another.
Peel back my skin and
you will find   barnacles cemented
                 to my spine, my scapula,
                 my sternum and my sphenoid.
                 compliance is embedded
                 in my skeleton.
My blood is   brackish
and my organs are
     wrapped in seaweed.
Break my bones and know
I will offer them as penance.

synecology

The school garden Mrs. B
started still stands.
I see the students topple over one
another, celebrating
their harvest. They keep expanding

the cemeteries in town, so I keep
my stereo turned all the way down
(it's the least a friend can do).
Sophie's parents sold their house
and my mother's place has changed
hands several times. Do the Arles still
live off Skeet Club? Or have they all
scattered like their father's ashes?
Kennedy's crash site is covered
in creeping phlox and
everyone remembered
her birthday last week.
Someone is angry I am writing
this poem, but it's time I forgive us both.

Is there a faerie portal off Eastchester?
Near the greenway? I'll check underneath
the tree I planted when I was six,
clean up the creek and
my own muddy waters.

I just want to go home.

Oh, Emerald Isle!

How I long for you!   The nation
        plunges into a week-long
        heatwave, and when it breaks,
        it will be by mere degrees.
I mist myself with cool water, pretending
to feel the ocean breeze from your cliffside.
Sometimes,   I transform
        the thrumming of the AC unit
        into a gentle, whooshing fjord.
My husband waters the plants   and
I close my tearful eyes, letting the damp moss
        transport me.   *Take me back,*
        I whisper,   *take me home.*
My chest remembers a time when my ancestors
breathed brine.   There is a hole where
        knowing you should be;
the hook threaded through it yanks me east,
but I force myself to kneel in the front yard.
The grass is barely hanging onto its green and
is reflecting the heat. I pretend it is the homeland
while I finish gardening.   The lilac Sea Aster
in front of the windows were planted for you.

Is it snowing where you are?
after Jean Webster

Are you headed to the cemetery
to listen to the winter birds?
How is your garlic growing? When
does your shift end? Are you planning
to rest for the rest of the week? What are
the kids' schemes for the season?
How do you imbue every moment
with self-care? Are the ghosts
fogging up your windows?
Is the dog snuggled beneath
the blanket with you? How are
your feet?   Weary?   Upbeat?
          Preparing to dance?
     Anticipating the global collapse?
There is an ache in my bones; it could mean
                              storms
but   it also might be my body whispering
                    I miss you.
Would you like to meet halfway,   find
a cabin in North Dakota,   and discover
new ways to unwind? Shed our exoskeletons
and anguish? Start a riot in our pajamas?
If we can't meet in the Midwest, then
are you free for a call tomorrow?
          Did it snow?
Is the sky covered in clouds, or
are we looking at the same stars?

crack open your ribs for me
after Carolyn Forché

Open your mouth   lover
but do not speak.
Swallow me whole;
I cling to your tastebuds,   fingers
cut on jagged molars   and
                       filled-in cavities.
    (let me live inside you)
Carolyn tore open the letters and
licked the envelope; I crawled
down your esophagus. Break me
apart, the bile in your belly bubbling
until I am metaphor   and nothing more
      (become me the way I will become you)

Unrealized

We stripped down to nothing before jumping in.
The ripples were gentle against my chest
as she swam closer, whispering,
> *If you didn't have a boyfriend right now,*
> *I would definitely kiss you.*
>
> She let her legs brush mine instead
> as she darted back out of grasp.
> Those same legs wrap themselves
>   around me as she falls asleep.

We're driving through Arapahoe   and   her hands find mine
> *I can't wait to go through*
> *my gay phase*
> *in college,*
> the hushed tone
> barely carried over the stereo.

I pull myself from my partner's arms at pride to answer her call -
Another man is late,   this time a decade older;
> she says she's not scared
> but her voice quivers
> in a way that tells me
> she is shaking

Breathe   *You don't have to do anything you don't want to -*
> *But I should want to,*

       that whine is intoxicating

No one stayed for our last goodbye,   packing up the car
       while she sobbed into my sweater
There was snow coating her hair   her lips were blue
       when she pressed them to my palm
Then there was a three-hour flight   and a surprise visit,
Embarrassment couldn't reach me, held up only by her embrace.
       Why are we crying?
       But she doesn't want to know the answer.

I pull a dress from the back of my closet and she gasps,
fingers hovering   (always hovering)   above the fabric.
       How did you find this?
       Her eyes become unfocused,
       honed in on a moment months ago
       at a vintage thrift store.
       I wish you could be my boyfriend.
Her hands cradle my face   in every picture I can find -
       We spent years simply holding one another.

beauty as an invasive species

a kudzu forest overtakes an abandoned
parking lot, swallowing rusted-out sedans
and the concrete jungle, choking out even
the most resilient native plants.
the wisteria blooms, strangling the trees
supporting them; the canopy shifts then
collapses, leaving gaps quickly filled
by dense thickets. if nature overtakes
itself, are we destined to overtake

each other?

erosion

She sweeps her curls
across her shoulder, and
the tendrils cling to my fingers.
Her muscles resist
the push of my hands;
I pull back
place a kiss
at the nape of her neck.
This will take time, I whisper.
the careful intimacy,
the throbbing ache of overuse,
the subtle give. This matter,
which cannot be destroyed,
has transformed us.
She runs over me,
water in a rocky creek
smoothing chipped edges
over centuries.
Time takes us, love, she murmurs.
My hands travel over mountains until
they intertwine with hers.
Death, my old friend,
has become unrecognizable;
the planet's implosion may take
our entire lifetime, but
the universe is still young.

I fold myself into
the cosmos, her arms.

Isn't it enough to see that a garden is beautiful
after Douglas Adams

without having to believe that there are
fairies at the bottom of it, too?
My lover wraps his arms around me, crushing
me into the couch cushions, my scowl dissolving
into laughter. My body falls back into the past,
summer rain against a warm lake. When my head
breaks the surface, it is sleeting; I shiver.
My toes graze the sandy bottom. He holds me
as the shudders subside, wiping the deluge
from beneath my eyes.   If only
there were life rafts
for the reservoirs of trauma.   If only
daisies beckoned
from the shoreline.   If only
the bank wasn't covered
in snow. The fae keep me up late, dancing
in a pool of my destruction; my lover
hangs on as I do somersaults through surrealism.
The fairies are having a ball at the bottom of the
lagoon,
whispering invitations I know will lead me astray.
I bolt the doors with iron, sheltering myself
in the harbor of my lover. We exist
in the crackle of a candle,
the light from the flame, the shadows on the wall;
we frolicked in the future, and I find him
strewn through every version.

<u>almost</u>

The first peach
of the season,
the burst of acidic florals
after a bland winter
overstayed its welcome.
The initial taste rushes in
with warmth   nearly forgotten,
a dream that escaped
as your eyelids open.

June harvests are delicious,
ripe with desperation,
        deprivation,
       denial.
When August arrives,
the flavor has deepened,
        holding bouquets while
        plunging off
        the end of the pier
        at high tide.

August boasts, filling
both our fridge and freezer
before spilling into a basket
for the neighbors.

How to be Human 101

I asked my stepmom
at what point did you finally figure it out?
All she does is shrug, saying *you don't.*
I can separate lights and brights, beat life
back into a breathless chest, keep a family
fed on debt. I know forgiving and
forgetting are usually busy avoiding one another,
that to survive is to lie, but to love
is to tell the truth; none of that taught me
how to keep you.
When will this all get easier?
Not the loving, but
      the living.
I place the weight of my palm in yours and whisper
    do you feel how much lighter my limbs are
    compared to the first day we met?
    Life is a fickle wind
    coming off the sea;
    sometimes we sway
    and other times we snap.
    We are no longer saplings;
    how difficult it would be   *to uproot us.*
    It might never be painless,   *but I am both*
                                        lighter
                                        and less afraid
                                        of being
                                        blown over.

When we die, can we become mycelium?

In constant communication?

A new form of regeneration?

I hope your consciousness remains
a constant companion.
This is not quite reincarnation, but
an unbecoming to become intertwined
with all that already exists.

My shoulders used to shudder at the thought of
smoldering into ash
or being packed beneath 2,597 pounds of earth.
Now I hope the same worm colony devours us,
that we are deposited
in the same soil so we can
sprout the same mushrooms,
feed the same flowers, and
nourish them into eternity.

<u>don't ever forget this breeze</u>

The air is crisp,   wind whipping
    at the baby hairs that wander
        from my bun.
Sweat coats every inch of my abdomen, and
still
I don't dare take off my jacket.
You amble along beside me,   oblivious.
We both slow at the bustle   at the peak,
everyone enthralled, eyeing the view from the
mountainside.
We hunker down between a boulder, a sapling,
and a cliff.
You huff at the idea of being surrounded, and I agree
        (though for very
        different reasons)
Can my palms get any slicker?
The chatter fades to crunching leaves, the smell
of nature narrowing until only your faint musk
enters my lungs. The rough rocks beneath my fingers
grow pliant. The breeze comes gently, willing me
                to breathe
"Will you let me learn to love you

forever?"

<u>You cannot lose what is a part of you</u>

We are a cosmo flower   in my palm.
    I shake   bumble   and   trip
        through the garden
Won't the petals fall off?   but you point out
    all the sprouts from last fall's blooms
(whatever we lose   comes back)
    I regret growing my garden in the sand,
    but we are creating compost from waste.
These things take time   you croon,
    but there is an ache where I miss you
        already   (whatever we lose
        comes back).
This poem is   a ghost   of an emotion
    an echo   -   would you
believe
    my love is evergreen? I foraged these feelings
    in a forest full of frost-hardy perennials.
    Fuck a ring, we have found faerie portals
    together. I don't need always, or answers
    (whatever we lose comes back).

A network of mycelium will connect us
until the planet implodes.
Spring is a million years in the making
    and this storm is mere weeks old.
We are made of oceans and fossils
roots   and   resistance.

Who is afraid
 of a little rain?
(Whatever we lose   remains
 a part of us).

This could be all we know of love
after Gregory Alan Isakov

and I would be grateful.
My touch-starved body arches
toward your palms automatically.
Soil cakes your calloused hands
and my fingertips knead the knots
in your shoulders. You spill
the contents of your day on my lap
and I lay your head atop it.
Rest now, I croon, *feel me
running through your hair.*
Years are lost to me, but
I know better than to go searching.
Love lives not in that foggy forest.
The past whispers, but you,
my love, beckon.   I come.
I always come back home,
back to you, back to reality,
back to the path, back
to myself. I always come back,
and you are always waiting. Please,
let this be all I know. I am so tired
of knowing anything else.

I'm sorry I didn't text you back
after R. K. Nightingale

I threw my phone in a lake and remembered
hands were for
more than wringing.
These hands wrote poems - on paper! -
and sealed letters in envelopes.
Have you checked your mail lately,
or were you resigned to receiving only junk?
Complacency has taken root in me,
and I let it. *I let it.*
The ground is all red clay and rocks,
but I dug out the submission
until my nail beds were bloody.
I wrote more poems, penned more letters.
My fingers ache but at least
I feel something. *I feel everything.*
Even in shallow waters, there is an undercurrent
of agony; it would be easy to surrender.
But then I remember how sunlight feels in the Spring.
I remember I have letters to write.

Have you checked your mail lately?

It's Raining, Let's Go Outside

Let's check on the plants.
Hold my hand.
I know we've never done it before, but
        what if I asked you to dance?
Let's get drenched, cling to one another like clothes.
Rest your hands heavy on my shoulders,
the weight of jeans against my skin;
I am soaked.
Unzip my attitude, slip into me,
        show me how to make this body
                a home.
I can't tell your fingers from water droplets,
I only know you are everywhere.
You smell like agave and dirt and
the rain smells like fresh chances and
            warmer weather.
I have never had love where
I was comfortable enough to belt out ballads
as the barrage beat down on me -
I have never had a love safe from the storm.
        I have never had love.

Come, dance with me in the deluge.

It is Spring and

my husband soaks his
seedlings, though he
would mention
nature cannot be
owned, only
tended to.
On warm days,
he sets them
on the back deck.
Instead of culling
the weakest plants,
he offers them
to the neighbors,
saying   *I am*
         as strong as this.
The cherry blossom
tree is in full bloom
and my palms are
covered in cool dirt.
It is spring and

this is enough.

Acknowledgements:

"crows hold grudges for 17 years" is an after of a poem by Cat Speranzini

"Winter took more than she needed" was a prompt by Amy R. (@daylily.poetry on Instagram)

"What if this soft body is prey?" is an after of Mary Oliver's poem "Wild Geese"

"I am terrified of weather because I see you when it rains" is an after of Noah Khan's song "Stick Season"

"Is it snowing where you are?" is an after of a poem by Jean Webster

"Crack open my ribs" references the line "I tore open your letter and licked the envelope's seal for any lingering taste of you" from *The Angel of History* by Carolyn Forché

"Isn't it enough to see that the garden is beautiful without having to believe that there are faeries at the bottom of it too?" is a quote by Douglas Adams and was a prompt from Carol J Forrester

"This could be all we know of love" is an after of Gregory Alan Isakov's song "Big Black Car."

"I'm sorry I didn't text you back" is an after of a poem by R. K. Nightengale

Thank you to the presses and editors who believed in these poems.

"crows hold grudges for 17 years" (Backwards Trajectory, 2025)

"What if this soft body is prey?" (Querencia Press, 2025)

"until death." (Querencia Press, 2025)

"My Fingers Ache From Holding On" (Wingless Dreamer, 2023)

"predator" *(Issue 16,* SCAB Magazine, 2025)

"Is it snowing where you are?" (Querencia Press, 2024)

"Unrealized" (*Issue 1*, By the Beach, 2024)

"erosion" (*Issue 12*, Transmuted, 2025)

"Isn't it enough to see that the garden is beautiful without having to believe that there are faeries at the bottom of it too?" (The Word's Faire, 2024)

"How to be Human 101" (Inlandia, 2023)

"When we die, can we become mycelium?" (*Not Ghosts, but Spirits*, Querencia Press, 2025)

"This could be all we know of love" (Querencia Press, 2024)

"It's Raining, Let's Go Outside" (Bowyer, Maggie, *Homecoming,* 2023) and (Wingless Dreamer, 2024)

"It is Spring and" (*ALBATROSS #32,* Anabiosis Press, 2025)